Quiet the mind & the soul will speak...

MEDITATION JOURNAL BELONGS TO:

Copyright Leska Hamaty
Whole Heart Paper Press

All rights reserved. In no way is it legal to reproduce, duplicate, or transmit any part of this document in either electronic means or in printed format. Recording of this publication is strictly prohibited and any storage of this document is not allowed unless given written permission from the publisher directly.

Cultivating a daily meditation practice is the journey of your soul. In this journey there is no right or wrong way, the only true necessary component is to get started.

This journal was created for those who may be looking to enhance their life by bringing in a daily meditation practice that has the potential to bring in a new depth of relaxation, alleviate pain and come to know a new level of awareness and clarity in all aspects of life.

We have all read the claims of change that meditation opens the door to but the only way to know this for yourself is to experience it with many types of meditation methods available today keeping a log will help you determine what works best for you.

Start with 10 minutes a day. Be silent, compassionate and be patient with yourself. Build one day at a time and track your progress.

> This is the gift
> you're giving
> yourself

DATE: TIME: DURATION:

LOCATION:

MEDITATION
  METHOD:

HOW I FEEL:
  BEFORE

HOW I FEEL:
  AFTER

NOTES:

DATE: TIME: DURATION:

LOCATION:

MEDITATION
   METHOD:

HOW I FEEL:
  BEFORE

HOW I FEEL:
  AFTER

NOTES:

DATE: TIME: DURATION:

LOCATION:

MEDITATION
   METHOD:

HOW I FEEL:
  BEFORE

HOW I FEEL:
  AFTER

NOTES:

DATE: TIME: DURATION:

LOCATION:

MEDITATION
  METHOD:

HOW I FEEL:
 BEFORE

HOW I FEEL:
 AFTER

NOTES:

DATE: TIME: DURATION:

LOCATION:

MEDITATION
  METHOD:

HOW I FEEL:
  BEFORE

HOW I FEEL:
  AFTER

NOTES:

DATE: TIME: DURATION:

LOCATION:

MEDITATION
METHOD:

HOW I FEEL:
BEFORE

HOW I FEEL:
AFTER

NOTES:

DATE: TIME: DURATION:

LOCATION:

MEDITATION
  METHOD:

HOW I FEEL:
  BEFORE

HOW I FEEL:
  AFTER

NOTES:

DATE: TIME: DURATION:

LOCATION:

MEDITATION
   METHOD:

HOW I FEEL:
  BEFORE

HOW I FEEL:
  AFTER

NOTES:

DATE: TIME: DURATION:

LOCATION:

MEDITATION
METHOD:

HOW I FEEL:
BEFORE

HOW I FEEL:
AFTER

NOTES:

DATE: TIME: DURATION:

LOCATION:

MEDITATION METHOD:

HOW I FEEL:
BEFORE

HOW I FEEL:
AFTER

NOTES:

DATE: TIME: DURATION:

LOCATION:

MEDITATION
  METHOD:

HOW I FEEL:
  BEFORE

HOW I FEEL:
  AFTER

NOTES:

DATE: TIME: DURATION:

LOCATION:

MEDITATION
   METHOD:

HOW I FEEL:
  BEFORE

HOW I FEEL:
  AFTER

NOTES:

DATE: TIME: DURATION:

LOCATION:

MEDITATION
  METHOD:

HOW I FEEL:
  BEFORE

HOW I FEEL:
  AFTER

NOTES:

DATE: TIME: DURATION:

LOCATION:

MEDITATION
  METHOD:

HOW I FEEL:
  BEFORE

HOW I FEEL:
  AFTER

NOTES:

DATE: TIME: DURATION:

LOCATION:

MEDITATION
  METHOD:

HOW I FEEL:
  BEFORE

HOW I FEEL:
  AFTER

NOTES:

DATE: TIME: DURATION:

LOCATION:

MEDITATION
   METHOD:

HOW I FEEL:
 BEFORE

___

HOW I FEEL:
 AFTER

___

NOTES:

DATE: TIME: DURATION:

LOCATION:

MEDITATION METHOD:

HOW I FEEL:
BEFORE

HOW I FEEL:
AFTER

NOTES:

DATE: TIME: DURATION:

LOCATION:

MEDITATION METHOD:

HOW I FEEL:
BEFORE

HOW I FEEL:
AFTER

NOTES:

DATE: TIME: DURATION:

LOCATION:

MEDITATION
   METHOD:

HOW I FEEL:
   BEFORE

HOW I FEEL:
   AFTER

NOTES:

DATE: TIME: DURATION:

LOCATION:

MEDITATION
  METHOD:

HOW I FEEL:
  BEFORE

HOW I FEEL:
  AFTER

NOTES:

| DATE: | TIME: | DURATION: |

LOCATION:

MEDITATION METHOD:

HOW I FEEL:
BEFORE

HOW I FEEL:
AFTER

NOTES:

DATE: **TIME:** **DURATION:**

LOCATION:

MEDITATION METHOD:

HOW I FEEL:
BEFORE

HOW I FEEL:
AFTER

NOTES:

DATE: **TIME:** **DURATION:**

LOCATION:

MEDITATION METHOD:

HOW I FEEL:
BEFORE

HOW I FEEL:
AFTER

NOTES:

DATE: TIME: DURATION:

LOCATION:

MEDITATION
  METHOD:

HOW I FEEL:
  BEFORE

HOW I FEEL:
  AFTER

NOTES:

DATE:	TIME:	DURATION:

LOCATION:

MEDITATION
  METHOD:

HOW I FEEL:
  BEFORE

HOW I FEEL:
  AFTER

NOTES:

DATE: **TIME:** **DURATION:**

LOCATION:

MEDITATION METHOD:

HOW I FEEL:
BEFORE

HOW I FEEL:
AFTER

NOTES:

DATE: TIME: DURATION:

LOCATION:

MEDITATION
  METHOD:

HOW I FEEL:
  BEFORE

HOW I FEEL:
  AFTER

NOTES:

DATE: **TIME:** **DURATION:**

LOCATION:

MEDITATION METHOD:

HOW I FEEL:
BEFORE

HOW I FEEL:
AFTER

NOTES:

DATE: **TIME:** **DURATION:**

LOCATION:

MEDITATION METHOD:

HOW I FEEL:
BEFORE

HOW I FEEL:
AFTER

NOTES:

DATE: TIME: DURATION:

LOCATION:

MEDITATION
  METHOD:

HOW I FEEL:
  BEFORE

HOW I FEEL:
  AFTER

NOTES:

DATE: TIME: DURATION:

LOCATION:

MEDITATION
  METHOD:

HOW I FEEL:
  BEFORE

HOW I FEEL:
  AFTER

NOTES:

DATE: **TIME:** **DURATION:**

LOCATION:

MEDITATION METHOD:

HOW I FEEL:
BEFORE

HOW I FEEL:
AFTER

NOTES:

DATE: TIME: DURATION:

LOCATION:

MEDITATION METHOD:

HOW I FEEL:
BEFORE

HOW I FEEL:
AFTER

NOTES:

DATE: TIME: DURATION:

LOCATION:

MEDITATION METHOD:

HOW I FEEL:
BEFORE

HOW I FEEL:
AFTER

NOTES:

DATE: TIME: DURATION:

LOCATION:

MEDITATION
  METHOD:

HOW I FEEL:
  BEFORE

HOW I FEEL:
  AFTER

NOTES:

DATE: TIME: DURATION:

LOCATION:

MEDITATION
    METHOD:

HOW I FEEL:
  BEFORE

HOW I FEEL:
  AFTER

NOTES:

DATE: TIME: DURATION:

LOCATION:

MEDITATION
   METHOD:

HOW I FEEL:
   BEFORE

HOW I FEEL:
   AFTER

NOTES:

DATE: TIME: DURATION:

LOCATION:

MEDITATION
   METHOD:

HOW I FEEL:
  BEFORE

HOW I FEEL:
  AFTER

NOTES:

DATE: TIME: DURATION:

LOCATION:

MEDITATION METHOD:

HOW I FEEL:
BEFORE

HOW I FEEL:
AFTER

NOTES:

DATE: TIME: DURATION:

LOCATION:

MEDITATION
  METHOD:

HOW I FEEL:
  BEFORE

HOW I FEEL:
  AFTER

NOTES:

DATE: TIME: DURATION:

LOCATION:

MEDITATION
  METHOD:

HOW I FEEL:
  BEFORE

HOW I FEEL:
  AFTER

NOTES:

DATE: TIME: DURATION:

LOCATION:

MEDITATION
   METHOD:

HOW I FEEL:
  BEFORE

HOW I FEEL:
  AFTER

NOTES:

DATE: TIME: DURATION:

LOCATION:

MEDITATION
   METHOD:

HOW I FEEL:
  BEFORE

HOW I FEEL:
  AFTER

NOTES:

DATE: TIME: DURATION:

LOCATION:

MEDITATION
  METHOD:

HOW I FEEL:
  BEFORE

HOW I FEEL:
  AFTER

NOTES:

DATE: TIME: DURATION:

LOCATION:

MEDITATION
  METHOD:

HOW I FEEL:
  BEFORE

HOW I FEEL:
  AFTER

NOTES:

DATE: TIME: DURATION:

LOCATION:

MEDITATION
METHOD:

HOW I FEEL:
BEFORE

HOW I FEEL:
AFTER

NOTES:

DATE: TIME: DURATION:

LOCATION:

MEDITATION
   METHOD:

HOW I FEEL:
  BEFORE

HOW I FEEL:
  AFTER

NOTES:

DATE: TIME: DURATION:

LOCATION:

MEDITATION METHOD:

HOW I FEEL:
BEFORE

HOW I FEEL:
AFTER

NOTES:

DATE: **TIME:** **DURATION:**

LOCATION:

MEDITATION METHOD:

HOW I FEEL:
BEFORE

HOW I FEEL:
AFTER

NOTES:

DATE: TIME: DURATION:

LOCATION:

MEDITATION
   METHOD:

HOW I FEEL:
   BEFORE

HOW I FEEL:
   AFTER

NOTES:

DATE: TIME: DURATION:

LOCATION:

MEDITATION
  METHOD:

HOW I FEEL:
  BEFORE

HOW I FEEL:
  AFTER

NOTES:

DATE: TIME: DURATION:

LOCATION:

MEDITATION
   METHOD:

HOW I FEEL:
  BEFORE

HOW I FEEL:
  AFTER

NOTES:

DATE: TIME: DURATION:

LOCATION:

MEDITATION
   METHOD:

HOW I FEEL:
  BEFORE

HOW I FEEL:
  AFTER

NOTES:

DATE: TIME: DURATION:

LOCATION:

MEDITATION
   METHOD:

HOW I FEEL:
  BEFORE

HOW I FEEL:
  AFTER

NOTES:

DATE:　　　　　　　　TIME:　　　　　　　　DURATION:

LOCATION:

MEDITATION
　METHOD:

HOW I FEEL:
　BEFORE

HOW I FEEL:
　AFTER

NOTES:

DATE: TIME: DURATION:

LOCATION:

MEDITATION
  METHOD:

HOW I FEEL:
  BEFORE

HOW I FEEL:
  AFTER

NOTES:

DATE:　　　　　　TIME:　　　　　　DURATION:

LOCATION:

MEDITATION
METHOD:

HOW I FEEL:
BEFORE

HOW I FEEL:
AFTER

NOTES:

DATE: TIME: DURATION:

LOCATION:

MEDITATION
METHOD:

HOW I FEEL:
BEFORE

HOW I FEEL:
AFTER

NOTES:

DATE: TIME: DURATION:

LOCATION:

MEDITATION METHOD:

HOW I FEEL:
BEFORE

HOW I FEEL:
AFTER

NOTES:

DATE: TIME: DURATION:

LOCATION:

MEDITATION
   METHOD:

HOW I FEEL:
  BEFORE

HOW I FEEL:
  AFTER

NOTES:

DATE: TIME: DURATION:

LOCATION:

MEDITATION
METHOD:

HOW I FEEL:
BEFORE

HOW I FEEL:
AFTER

NOTES:

DATE: TIME: DURATION:

LOCATION:

MEDITATION
  METHOD:

HOW I FEEL:
  BEFORE

HOW I FEEL:
  AFTER

NOTES:

DATE: TIME: DURATION:

LOCATION:

MEDITATION
  METHOD:

HOW I FEEL:
  BEFORE

HOW I FEEL:
  AFTER

NOTES:

DATE: TIME: DURATION:

LOCATION:

MEDITATION
METHOD:

HOW I FEEL:
BEFORE

HOW I FEEL:
AFTER

NOTES:

DATE: TIME: DURATION:

LOCATION:

MEDITATION METHOD:

HOW I FEEL:
BEFORE

HOW I FEEL:
AFTER

NOTES:

DATE: TIME: DURATION:

LOCATION:

MEDITATION METHOD:

HOW I FEEL:
BEFORE

HOW I FEEL:
AFTER

NOTES:

DATE: TIME: DURATION:

LOCATION:

MEDITATION METHOD:

HOW I FEEL:
BEFORE

HOW I FEEL:
AFTER

NOTES:

DATE: TIME: DURATION:

LOCATION:

MEDITATION
   METHOD:

HOW I FEEL:
  BEFORE

HOW I FEEL:
  AFTER

NOTES:

DATE: TIME: DURATION:

LOCATION:

MEDITATION METHOD:

HOW I FEEL:
BEFORE

HOW I FEEL:
AFTER

NOTES:

DATE: TIME: DURATION:

LOCATION:

MEDITATION
   METHOD:

HOW I FEEL:
  BEFORE

HOW I FEEL:
  AFTER

NOTES:

DATE:　　　　　　　　TIME:　　　　　　　　DURATION:

LOCATION:

MEDITATION
　METHOD:

HOW I FEEL:
 BEFORE

HOW I FEEL:
 AFTER

NOTES:

DATE: TIME: DURATION:

LOCATION:

MEDITATION
  METHOD:

HOW I FEEL:
  BEFORE

HOW I FEEL:
  AFTER

NOTES:

DATE:　　　　　　TIME:　　　　　　DURATION:

LOCATION:

MEDITATION
　METHOD:

HOW I FEEL:
　BEFORE

HOW I FEEL:
　AFTER

NOTES:

DATE: TIME: DURATION:

LOCATION:

MEDITATION
   METHOD:

HOW I FEEL:
  BEFORE

HOW I FEEL:
  AFTER

NOTES:

DATE: TIME: DURATION:

LOCATION:

MEDITATION
   METHOD:

HOW I FEEL:
  BEFORE

HOW I FEEL:
  AFTER

NOTES:

DATE: TIME: DURATION:

LOCATION:

MEDITATION
   METHOD:

HOW I FEEL:
  BEFORE

HOW I FEEL:
  AFTER

NOTES:

DATE:　　　　　　　　TIME:　　　　　　　　DURATION:

LOCATION:

MEDITATION
　METHOD:

HOW I FEEL:
　BEFORE

HOW I FEEL:
　AFTER

NOTES:

DATE: TIME: DURATION:

LOCATION:

MEDITATION
   METHOD:

HOW I FEEL:
  BEFORE

HOW I FEEL:
  AFTER

NOTES:

DATE: TIME: DURATION:

LOCATION:

MEDITATION
   METHOD:

HOW I FEEL:
  BEFORE

HOW I FEEL:
  AFTER

NOTES:

DATE: TIME: DURATION:

LOCATION:

MEDITATION
   METHOD:

HOW I FEEL:
  BEFORE

HOW I FEEL:
  AFTER

NOTES:

DATE: TIME: DURATION:

LOCATION:

MEDITATION METHOD:

HOW I FEEL:
BEFORE

HOW I FEEL:
AFTER

NOTES:

DATE: TIME: DURATION:

LOCATION:

MEDITATION
    METHOD:

HOW I FEEL:
  BEFORE

HOW I FEEL:
  AFTER

NOTES:

DATE: TIME: DURATION:

LOCATION:

MEDITATION METHOD:

HOW I FEEL:
BEFORE

HOW I FEEL:
AFTER

NOTES:

DATE: TIME: DURATION:

LOCATION:

MEDITATION
   METHOD:

HOW I FEEL:
   BEFORE

HOW I FEEL:
   AFTER

NOTES:

DATE: TIME: DURATION:

LOCATION:

MEDITATION
METHOD:

HOW I FEEL:
BEFORE

HOW I FEEL:
AFTER

NOTES:

DATE:　　　　　　　TIME:　　　　　　　DURATION:

LOCATION:

MEDITATION
   METHOD:

HOW I FEEL:
   BEFORE

HOW I FEEL:
   AFTER

NOTES:

DATE: TIME: DURATION:

LOCATION:

MEDITATION METHOD:

HOW I FEEL:
BEFORE

HOW I FEEL:
AFTER

NOTES:

DATE: TIME: DURATION:

LOCATION:

MEDITATION
  METHOD:

HOW I FEEL:
  BEFORE

HOW I FEEL:
  AFTER

NOTES:

DATE: **TIME:** **DURATION:**

LOCATION:

MEDITATION METHOD:

HOW I FEEL:
BEFORE

HOW I FEEL:
AFTER

NOTES:

DATE: TIME: DURATION:

LOCATION:

MEDITATION
  METHOD:

HOW I FEEL:
  BEFORE

HOW I FEEL:
  AFTER

NOTES:

DATE: TIME: DURATION:

LOCATION:

MEDITATION
  METHOD:

HOW I FEEL:
  BEFORE

HOW I FEEL:
  AFTER

NOTES:

DATE: TIME: DURATION:

LOCATION:

MEDITATION
  METHOD:

HOW I FEEL:
  BEFORE

HOW I FEEL:
  AFTER

NOTES:

DATE: TIME: DURATION:

LOCATION:

MEDITATION METHOD:

HOW I FEEL:
BEFORE

HOW I FEEL:
AFTER

NOTES:

DATE: TIME: DURATION:

LOCATION:

MEDITATION
   METHOD:

HOW I FEEL:
  BEFORE

HOW I FEEL:
  AFTER

NOTES:

DATE: TIME: DURATION:

LOCATION:

MEDITATION METHOD:

HOW I FEEL:
BEFORE

HOW I FEEL:
AFTER

NOTES:

DATE:　　　　　　　　TIME:　　　　　　　　DURATION:

LOCATION:

MEDITATION
　METHOD:

HOW I FEEL:
　BEFORE

HOW I FEEL:
　AFTER

NOTES:

DATE: TIME: DURATION:

LOCATION:

MEDITATION
  METHOD:

HOW I FEEL:
  BEFORE

HOW I FEEL:
  AFTER

NOTES:

DATE: TIME: DURATION:

LOCATION:

MEDITATION
   METHOD:

HOW I FEEL:
  BEFORE

HOW I FEEL:
  AFTER

NOTES:

DATE: TIME: DURATION:

LOCATION:

MEDITATION METHOD:

HOW I FEEL:
BEFORE

HOW I FEEL:
AFTER

NOTES:

DATE: TIME: DURATION:

LOCATION:

MEDITATION
   METHOD:

HOW I FEEL:
  BEFORE

HOW I FEEL:
  AFTER

NOTES:

Made in the USA
Middletown, DE
26 August 2019